Princess Diana

A Little Golden Book® Biography

By Sonali Fry

Illustrated by Hollie Hibbert

 A GOLDEN BOOK • NEW YORK

Text copyright © 2024 by Sonali Fry
Cover art and interior illustrations copyright © 2024 by Hollie Hibbert
All rights reserved. Published in the United States by Golden Books, an imprint of
Random House Children's Books, a division of Penguin Random House LLC, 1745 Broadway,
New York, NY 10019. Golden Books, A Golden Book, A Little Golden Book, the G colophon,
and the distinctive gold spine are registered trademarks of Penguin Random House LLC.
rhcbooks.com
Educators and librarians, for a variety of teaching tools, visit us at RHTeachersLibrarians.com
Library of Congress Control Number: 2023938877
ISBN 978-0-593-70385-4 (trade) — ISBN 978-0-593-70386-1 (ebook)
Printed in the United States of America
10 9 8 7 6 5 4 3 2

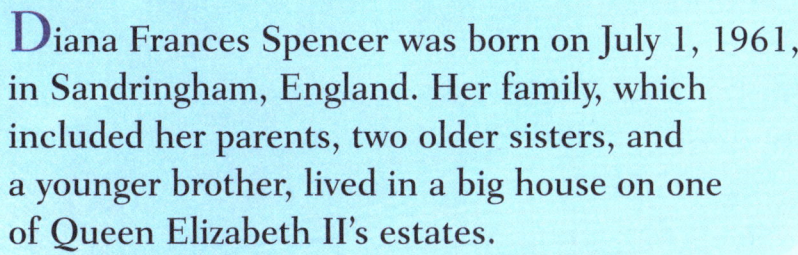

Diana Frances Spencer was born on July 1, 1961, in Sandringham, England. Her family, which included her parents, two older sisters, and a younger brother, lived in a big house on one of Queen Elizabeth II's estates.

When Diana was still in primary school, her parents got divorced. Her mother moved out of their home, and Diana only saw her on weekends. This made her very sad.

Diana enjoyed riding her bike and playing with her little brother and their pets. They had hamsters, rabbits, a cat named Marmalade, and a guinea pig named Peanuts.

At school, Diana was an average student, but she was very good at sports, music, and dance. She became a talented pianist and especially loved ballet, practicing whenever she could.

When Diana was thirteen, her father inherited a mansion in the English countryside. Their new home had thirty-one bedrooms—and plenty of space for Diana to dance!

Her father also inherited a new title and was now Earl Spencer. Diana and her siblings got new titles, too. Diana was now Lady Spencer.

Diana moved to London when she turned eighteen and shared an apartment with some friends. She worked as a nanny and an assistant kindergarten teacher. Diana loved children—and they loved her.

In 1980, Diana began dating Prince Charles, the oldest son of Queen Elizabeth II. Charles would be king one day, and whoever he married would be queen!

Diana and Charles got to know each other over many phone calls. Charles also invited Diana to evenings at the opera and dinners at Buckingham Palace, the home of the royal family.

Soon, reporters realized that Prince Charles had a new girlfriend. They started following Diana everywhere she went, and her picture ended up in all the newspapers. Diana didn't like the attention, but she was falling in love with Charles. She knew that being with a prince meant being in the public eye.

After just a few months, Prince Charles asked Diana to marry him. She said yes! When they announced their big news on February 24, 1981, the whole world got a glimpse of her stunning sapphire engagement ring.

Diana got right to work and prepared for life as a princess. There were so many things she had to learn. Diana was given "princess lessons" and taught the proper way to wave, sit, bow, curtsy, and hold a teacup. Being a princess is harder than it sounds!

Soon, the big day arrived!

On July 29, 1981, Lady Diana Spencer married His Royal Highness the Prince of Wales in St. Paul's Cathedral in London. It was a grand ceremony with about 2,500 guests. Another 750 million people watched on television.

Diana's gown was one of the fanciest wedding dresses people had seen. It was embroidered with sequins, lace, and 10,000 pearls. The veil that was attached to her tiara was 459 feet long!

After the ceremony, Diana and Charles left the church in a horse-drawn carriage. Everyone hoped their life would be a fairy tale, like their wedding.

Diana now had the title Her Royal Highness the Princess of Wales. As a member of the royal family, her days were filled with meetings, parties, speeches, and other official duties.

A few months after their wedding, Diana and Charles were thrilled to find out they would be parents. In 1982, their son Prince William was born, followed by Prince Harry two years later.

Diana loved being a mother and changed the way royal children were raised. Until then, nannies had cared for the kids, but Diana believed that "a mother's arms are more comforting than anyone else's." She took her young sons along on royal business trips, and when the boys started school, she dropped them off and picked them up herself. She also showered them with affection, often kissing and hugging them in public.

Diana tried her best to protect her children from the media, but it got harder and harder. She had become a fashion trendsetter, and soon, she was the most photographed person in the world!

The public loved to see the fancy outfits she wore to different events, and designers copied her dresses because so many people wanted to look like her. Diana's fans also noticed when she changed her hairstyle, and many changed theirs to match hers.

While she didn't like the constant media attention, the woman who was once known as "Shy Di" used her fame to bring awareness to charities and organizations that helped improve lives. The ones especially close to her heart promoted the banning of landmines and helping people who are homeless as well as those with HIV/AIDS.

During her many visits to hospitals and schools, Diana became known for spending hours talking to people and listening to their stories. She truly cared and tried to help all those in need.

Diana wanted her sons to know what the world was like outside of the royal family. She said, "I want my boys to have an understanding of people's emotions, their insecurities . . . and their hopes and dreams." Diana often took William and Harry with her when she visited hospitals, homeless shelters, and orphanages. She longed for them to experience a "normal life," so they sometimes took public transportation around London.

In 1995, after fifteen years of marriage, Diana and Charles divorced. Diana knew she'd never be queen, but this didn't matter to her. Instead, she said she'd like to be "a queen of people's hearts."

Sadly, on August 31, 1997, Diana died in a car accident in Paris. The whole world mourned. People left about sixty million flowers at various memorials throughout London, including Kensington Palace, where she lived.

On the day of her funeral, one million people
stood on the streets of London to say goodbye to their
princess, and over two billion people watched on TV.

Diana made a lasting impact on her family and the world. As prime minister Tony Blair said, "She was the people's princess, and that is how she will stay. . . ."

Today, Diana's legacy lives on in her children. Prince William and Prince Harry have their own families now, and they continue to do the charity work that was so dear to their mother. Diana's kindness and compassion will never be forgotten, and she will forever be remembered as the queen of people's hearts.